Read-About® Geography

Colorado

By Cynthia Walker

Consultant
Nanci R. Vargus, Ed.D.
Assistant Professor of Literacy
University of Indianapolis
Indianapolis, Indiana

Children's Press®
A Division of Scholastic Inc.
New York   Toronto   London   Auckland   Sydney
Mexico City   New Delhi   Hong Kong
Danbury, Connecticut

Designer: Herman Adler Design
Photo Researcher: Caroline Anderson
The photo on the cover shows Mount Sneffels Wilderness Area, near
Telluride, Colorado.

Library of Congress Cataloging-in-Publication Data

Walker, Cynthia.
  Colorado / by Cynthia Walker.
      p. cm. – (Rookie read-about geography)
  Includes index.
  Summary: Introduces the geography, wildlife, and people of the state
of Colorado.
  ISBN 0-516-22735-1 (lib. bdg.)   0-516-27944-0 (pbk.)
  1. Colorado–Juvenile literature. 2. Colorado–Geography–Juvenile
literature. [1. Colorado.] I. Title. II. Series.
  F776.3.W35 2004
  917.8'8–dc22
                                          2003016932

CHILDREN'S PRESS, and ROOKIE READ-ABOUT®,
and associated logos are trademarks and or registered trademarks
of Scholastic Library Publishing. SCHOLASTIC and associated logos
are trademarks and or registered trademarks of Scholastic Inc.

1 2 3 4 5 6 7 8 9 10 R 13 12 11 10 09 08 07 06 05 04

Do you know which state is the highest?

Colorado is the highest state! It has many tall mountains.

Can you find Colorado on this map? It is shaped like a rectangle.

CANADA

WASHINGTON
OREGON
IDAHO
MONTANA
NORTH DAKOTA
SOUTH DAKOTA
WYOMING
MINNESOTA
WISCONSIN
MICHIGAN
NEVADA
UTAH
COLORADO
NEBRASKA
IOWA
ILLINOIS
INDIANA
OHIO
PENNSYLVANIA
CALIFORNIA
ARIZONA
NEW MEXICO
KANSAS
MISSOURI
KENTUCKY
WEST VIRGINIA
VIRGINIA
OKLAHOMA
ARKANSAS
TENNESSEE
NORTH CAROLINA
NEW HAMPSHIRE
VERMONT
MAINE
NEW YORK
MASSACHUSETTS
RHODE ISLAND
CONNECTICUT
NEW JERSEY
DELAWARE
MARYLAND
Washington, D.C.
TEXAS
LOUISIANA
MISSISSIPPI
ALABAMA
GEORGIA
SOUTH CAROLINA
FLORIDA

ALASKA
CANADA
MEXICO
HAWAII

North
West
East
South

5

Colorado is a state of
mountains, canyons,
and plains.

A canyon is a narrow
valley between mountains.
It has high, steep sides.

The mountains in Colorado are called the Rocky Mountains.

The highest mountain is Mount Elbert. It is 14,433 feet tall.

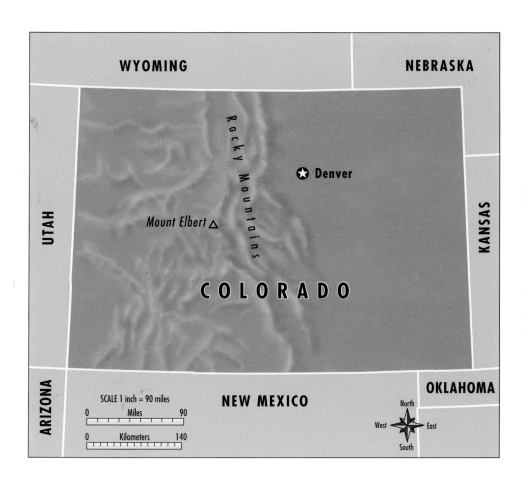

WYOMING

NEBRASKA

UTAH

KANSAS

Rocky Mountains

★ Denver

Mount Elbert △

C O L O R A D O

ARIZONA

SCALE 1 inch = 90 miles

0   Miles   90

0   Kilometers   140

NEW MEXICO

OKLAHOMA

North

West ✦ East

South

9

14

Colorado has a long
stretch of land called
the Continental Divide.

It separates the Rocky
Mountains into eastern
and western slopes.

In the 1800's, Colorado had a gold rush. Many people came to look for gold in the mountains.

Some of these miners made Colorado their home.

Denver

Denver is Colorado's largest city. It is also the state capital.

Other large cities in Colorado are Colorado Springs and Lakewood.

In Colorado, some people are park rangers and firefighters. Others work in offices, factories, and hospitals.

Firefighters

Colorado has farms and ranches. Farmers grow wheat, corn, fruits, and vegetables.

Ranchers raise cattle for beef.

Bighorn sheep, mountain lions, and other wild animals live in Colorado.

Bighorn sheep

The state bird is the
lark bunting.

Colorado has snowy winters and sunny summers.

The mountains and High Plains get the most snow. Many people visit Colorado in winter to go skiing.

These children are visiting the Dinosaur Discovery Museum.

There is so much to see and do in Colorado.

Words You Know

bighorn sheep

canyon

Colorado River

Denver

lark bunting

skiing

Index

animals, 23, 24–25
bighorn sheep, 24
canyons, 7
cattle, 23
cities, 19
Colorado River, 11
Colorado Springs, 19
Continental Divide, 15
Denver, 18,19
Dinosaur Discovery Museum, 29
farms, 22
firefighters, 20
fishing, 12
gold, 16
Grand Lake, 12
High Plains, 26
lakes, 12

Lakewood, 19
lark bunting, 25
Mount Elbert, 8
mountain lions, 24
mountains, 4, 7, 8, 15, 16, 26
museums, 29
plains, 7, 26
ranches, 22, 23
rivers, 11
Rocky Mountains, 8, 15
skiing, 26
state bird, 25
state capital, 19
streams, 12
summer, 26
winter, 26

About the Author

Cynthia Walker is an author and illustrator of children's books. She lives in New York. During one vacation, she traveled to the southwestern United States. She saw the beautiful Rocky Mountains there.

Photo Credits

Photographs © 2004: Dembinsky Photo Assoc.: 13 (Patti McConville), 25, 31 bottom left (Gary Meszaros), 6, 30 top right (G. Alan Nelson), 10, 30 bottom (Scott T. Smith); Hulton | Archive/Getty Images: 17; Network Aspen: 3, 28 (Jeffrey Aaronson), 27, 31 bottom right (Brian Bailey), 24, 30 top left (Michael Brands), 18, 31 top (Rebecca Green), 22 (Michael Lewis), 23 (John Russell); Viesti Collection, Inc.: cover (Richard Genova), 21 (Robert Winslow); Visuals Unlimited/Science: 14.

Maps by Bob Italiano